ASSURANCE

of your

CALLING

Study Manual

Rev. Celeste B. Atkins, Ph. D

ISBN 978-1-93574-124-4

ACKNOWLEDGEMENT

I dedicate this handbook to the many men and women who have been called by God into the ministry of Jesus Christ. As you go through this workbook, I want to inspire you to listen to the voice of God and follow His plan for your life and the ministry that He equipped you to do.

INTRODUCTION

This handbook is perfect for those who are unsure about their calling and who want to learn about God's calling on their lives. This material is designed to assist with recognizing gifts and callings that could be dominant or that you didn't realize were operating in your life. This information is based solely on scripture to give every believer the assurance and confidence to walk in their election and calling. We are trying to base our spiritual positions on what people say but focusing on the things that God placed in you before the foundation of this world. There is only one of you. Utilize everything that was divinely given to you.

CONTENTS

CHAPTER 1

The Basics

God does not equip those who are qualified, but He equips those He calls. I am confident that every person can identify people in ministry who thrive and those in ministry who seem to fail miserably. Did you ever consider that those failing are in the wrong position within the Body of Christ, and will succeed when they are placed in their God-assigned position?

One of the most fascinating stories in the Bible is the story of Gideon. Gideon served as the fifth major judge over Israel. You can read about Gideon in Judges 6 to 8. The Bible says that the children of Israel did evil in the sight of God and as a result of their evil, God delivered them into the hand of Midian for seven years. Many nations came against Israel and caused them great hardship. The children of Israel cried day and night unto the Lord. God first send a prophet and reminded the children of Israel how He brought them up from Egypt, delivered them out of the hand of the Egyptians, and out of bondage. They were oppressed in Egypt and God brought them out and gave them their land. The Bible say despite all that God did for them, they didn't obey God.

Our God is merciful, and He forgives us when man can't. The Bible goes on to say that the angel of the Lord, sat under an oak which was in Ophrah, where Gideon the son of Joash the Abiezrite threshed wheat by the winepress. He was in hiding from the Midianites. The angel of the Lord appeared to Gideon and according to scripture said, "The Lord is with thee, thou mighty man of valour." Gideon answered and said, "Oh my Lord, if the Lord be with us, why then is all this befallen us? And where be all His miracles which our fathers told us of, saying, Did not the Lord bring us up from Egypt? But now the Lord hath forsaken us, and delivered us into the hands of the Midianites." (Judges 6:11-13)

The Bible declares that the Lord looked at Gideon and said, "Go in this thy might, and thou shalt save Israel from the hand of the Midianites: have not I sent thee?" Gideon proceeded to tell God why he was not the person to save Israel from the hands of their enemies. He told God what He already knew about him, but God assured Gideon that because He called him, he would be with him, and let him know he at the leadership of God would smite the Midianites.

Gideon like all of us, couldn't see himself doing this task. He asked God to give him a sign. God honored his request. God knew that Gideon was afraid. He assured Gideon that He was with him, and that Gideon wouldn't die. The Bible says Gideon built an altar unto the Lord and called it Jehovahshalom. God was true to his word.

The purpose of this workbook is to help every doubtful, stagnant, and believer to make their election and call sure. The assignments are designed to assist in finding your rightful place in ministry and to expand the kingdom of God. When you are positioned in the wrong place you are wasting time and causing more harm than good. Let's begin by learning the basics of our gifts and callings.

2 Peter 1:10-11 **Wherefore the rather, brethren, give diligence to make our calling and election sure: for if ye do these things, ye shall never fail.**

What are your thoughts? _____

_____

_____

_____

_____

_____

The scripture confirms that when you are confident in your divine position and know your calling, you will not fail, you can't fail. Why? Because God positioned you and no one can take that from you. It is only when you attempt to position yourself, allow people to place you in the incorrect position. God doesn't bless you where you think you should be, He blesses you where He called you to be. The biggest confirmation is the success, growth, and impact. This assurance is not based on monetary dollars but on souls being saved, lives being changed, and the growth of each believer. Therefore, let's begin to make sure we have the assurance of our calling and our election.

A close relationship with God is important to discovering the revelation of all the gifts and callings of God in your life. The closer you feel you are to God the closer you need to be. Therefore, there are 3 principles that you must adopt in your life. If you make these principles a way of life, you will never bow to defeat, retreat in battle, or stray from God's purpose for your life to achieve spiritual success. The 3 basics are prayer, fasting, and staying in God's word. Let's examine the impact of each principle.

PRAYER - CONSTANT COMMUNICATION WITH GOD

Prayer causes us to engage in fellowship and communion with our God. God is our Commander-in-Chief. We get our instructions from Him. To many people are failing because they are listening to people and not God The Bible lets us know He speaks in a still small voice. Remember when God spoke to Elijah?

I Kings 19:11-13 And He said, God forth, and stand upon the mount before the Lord; And, behold, the Lord passed by, and a great and strong wind rent the mountains, and brake in pieces the rocks before the Lord; but the Lord was not in the wind: and after the wind an earthquake, but the Lord was not in the earthquake. And after the earthquake a fire; but the Lord was not in the fire: and after the fire a still small voice. And it was so, when Elijah heard it, that he wrapped his face in his mantle, and went out, and stood in the entering in of the cave. And, behold, there came a voice unto him, and said, What doest thou here, Elijah?

There are over sixty scriptures in the Old and New Testament that provide every believer with the impact of prayer, what to expect from praying to God, and the importance of praying to our Father in Heaven. Jesus even gave us a model prayer. **Read Matthew 6:9-13.**

Prayer is so important. This principle is one of our spiritual warfare weapons. Let's search the scripture to see the impact of having a prayer life.

Psalm 18:6 In my distress I called upon the Lord and cried unto my God; He heard my voice out of His temple, and my cry came before Him, even into His ears.

Matthew 18:20 For where two or three are gathered together in my name, there am I in the midst of them.

I John 5:14 And this is the confidence that we have in Him, that, if we ask any thing according to His will, He heareth us.

Colossians 4:2 Continue in prayer, and watch in the same with thanksgiving.

Matthew 6:5-8 And when thou prayest, thou shall not be as the hypocrites are: for they love to pray standing in the synagogues and in the corners of the streets, that they may be seen of men. Verily I say unto you, They have their reward. But thou, when thou prayest, enter into thy closet, and when thou hast shut thy door, pray to thy Father which is in secret; and thy Father which seeth in secret shall reward thee openly. But when ye pray, use not vain repetitions, as the heathen do: for they think that they shall be heard for their much speaking. Be not ye therefore like unto them: for your Father knoweth what things ye have need of, before ye ask him.

I Thessalonians 5:17 Pray without ceasing. In every thing give thanks: for this is the will of God in Christ Jesus concerning you.

Philippians 4:6 Be careful for nothing; but in every thing by prayer and supplication with thanksgiving let your requests be made known unto God.

How has a life of prayer changed your destiny? _____

_____

_____

2) FASTING – DENYING YOURSELF AND HUMBLING YOUR SPIRIT

Fasting is sustaining from food or something else. You are denying yourself and invoking the power of God. There are spiritual things that the natural man can never handle. Fasting is fighting spiritually.

Isaiah 58:6 **Is not this the fast that I have chosen? To loose the bands of wickedness, to undo the heavy burdens, and to let the oppressed go free, and that ye break every yoke?**

Matthew 6:16-18 **Moreover when ye fast, be not as the hypocrites, of a sad countenance: for they disfigure their faces, that they may appear unto men to fast. Verily I say unto you, they have their reward. But thou, when thou fastest, anoint thine head, and wash thy face: That thou appear not unto men to fast, but unto thy father which is in secret: and thy Father, which seeth in secret, shall reward thee openly.**

What benefits have your received by fasting? _____

_____

_____

_____

_____

_____

3) STAY IN THE WORD OF GOD - FORTIFYING YOUR SPIRITUAL MAN

The word of God is your spiritual food that feeds your spiritual man. If you don't eat daily, then you grow weak and if you are weak you become vulnerable to the attacks of the devil. To remain ready for service and ready for battle, you must stay in the word of God.

Psalms 40:7-9 Then said I, Lo, I come in the volume of the book it is written or me, I delight to do thy will, O my God: Yea, thy law is within my heart.

Psalms 119:11 Thy word have I hid in mine heart, that I might not sin against thee.

Psalms 119:105 Thy word is a lamp unto my feet, and a light unto my path.

John 15:4 Abide in me, and I in you. As the branch cannot bear fruit of itself, except it abide in the vine; no more can ye, except ye abide in me.

John 15:7 If ye abide in me, and my words abide in you, ye shall ask what ye will, and it shall be done unto you.

Hebrews 10:7 Then said I, Lo, I come (in the volume of the book it is written of me,) to do thy will, O God.

In what way has the word transformed your life in Christ Jesus? _____

_____

_____

_____

_____

_____

The next 2 principles are just as important as prayer, fasting, and staying in God's word. They are important because they can hinder your spiritual growth and keep you alienated from God. Many modern Christians don't speak of these next two principles, but for the sake of making our election and calling sure, we must cover them. Here they are:

4) REPENT

The definition of repent is to feel or express sincere regret or remorse about your wrongdoing or sin. True repentance is an inner change of heart that produces the fruits of a new behavior. A truly sorrowful person acts differently, speaks differently, and lives differently. This is the outward evidence of the inward change that is brought on by repentance. Let's see what the Bible says about repentance.

Joel 2:13 **And rend your heart, and not your garments, and turn unto the Lord your God: for He is gracious and merciful, slow to anger, and of great kindness, and repenteth him of the evil.**

Matthew 4:17 **From that time Jesus began to preach, and to say, Repent: for the kingdom of heaven is at hand.**

Matthew 9:13 **But go ye and learn what that meaneth, I will have mercy, and not sacrifice: for I am not come to call the righteous, but sinners to repentance.**

Revelation 3:19 As many as I love, I rebuke and chasten: be zealous therefore, and repent.

How has repentance made a difference in our life? _____

_____

_____

_____

_____

_____

_____

_____

5) FORGIVE

Forgiving others is letting go of resentment and giving up any claim to be compensated for the hurt or loss we have suffered. Forgiveness teaches us that love is unselfish, and it doesn't keep a record of wrongdoings. This is to free the person holding the grudge. You have to be free in order to hear from God.

Matthew 6:14 **For if ye forgive men their trespasses, your heavenly Father will also forgive you.**

Matthew 18:21-22 **Then came Peter to Him, and said, Lord, how oft shall my brother sin against me, and I forgive him? Till seven times? Jesus said unto him, I say not unto thee, until seven time: but, until seventy times seven.**

Ephesians 4:32 **And be ye kind one to another, tenderhearted, forgiving one another, even as God for Christ's sake hath forgiven you.**

Colossians 3:13 **Forbearing one another, and forgiving one another, if any man have a quarrel against any: even as Christ forgave you, so also do ye.**

Why is forgiveness powerful? _____

_____

HOMEWORK

1. Talking to God (Prayer)

    a.   Do you talk to God regularly?   _____ Yes   _____ No

    b.   Do you have a prayer partner?   _____ Yes   _____ No

    c.   Do you participate in a prayer line?   _____ Yes   _____ No

    d.   How many times a day do you pray alone? _____

    e.   How often do you pray with a prayer partner? _____

    f.   How often do you pray with a group? _____

Tell us about your prayer life. _____

_____

_____

_____

_____

FASTING

2. You Must Fast

    a.   Do you fast?   _____ Yes   _____ No

b. How often do you fast? _____

c. Do you fast with a group or when someone asks you to fast, or do you fast alone? _____ Yes _____ No

d. Do you wait for God to lead you to fast? _____ Yes _____ No

Tell us about your fasting life. _____

_____

_____

_____

_____

_____

_____

THE WORD OF GOD

3. Being in the Word of God is extremely important. You must read the Old and New Testaments. It can be on your own or with others. Studying is important to your growth. God speaks to you through His word.

a. Do you read something in God's Word daily? _____ Yes _____ No

b. Do you study God's Word on your own? _____ Yes _____ No

c. What is your favorite passage of scripture? _____

d. Have you ever heard the voice of God? _____ Yes _____ No

e. Do you write scriptures on postcards? _____ Yes _____ No

Share if you have ever heard the voice of God. _____

_____

_____

_____

_____

_____

_____

REPENT

4. Now that you read what the Bible says about repentance, answer the following questions?

a. Have you ever repent- _____ Yes   _____ No
   ed?

b. How often do you   _____
   repent?

c. Do you understand the _____ Yes   _____ No
   importance of repen-
   tance?

d. Are there any things   _____ Yes   _____ No
   you feel you must re-
   pent for now?

e. If you answered yes to
   question d, please do so
   now!

Locate a scripture that have not been mentioned on repentance. _____

_____

_____

_____

_____

_____

_____

_____

FORGIVENESS

5. Now that you recognize the importance of forgiving others, answer the following questions.

a. Are there people you haven't forgiven for their wrongdoings toward you or your family?   _____ Yes   _____ No

b. Have you every prayed and asked God for a forgiving spirit?   _____ Yes   _____ No

c. Are you willing to let go of all and any unforgiveness?   _____ Yes   _____ No

Locate a scripture that has not been mentioned on forgiveness. _____

_____

_____

_____

_____

_____

APPLICATION

Why is prayer, fasting, repentance, and forgiveness important to your growth in ministry? _____

_____

_____

_____

_____

_____

_____

_____

Read Judges 6 to 8 and write how the story of Gideon applies to your life and God's ministry. Write one to two pages.

CHAPTER 2

Foundational Ministry Calls

Now that we have established the basic principles, we must look at the foundational calls of being effective in the ministry of Jesus Christ. The Bible mentions several different "calls." They are mentioned in order of importance. Without the process of hearing, listening, and accepting each call, you can't be effective and be empowered for kingdom work.

The Apostle Paul has been regarded as one of the most influential figures of the Gospel. He founded several churches in Asia Minor and Europe. He used his positioning in life as a Jew and a Roman citizen to counsel to both Jews, Romans, and gentiles. We must remember Paul had to have a conversion experience. Before Paul gave his life to God, he persecuted the church and condemned many Christians to death. The Bible tells us about Paul's conversion experience in the Book of Acts. At the time his name was Saul, and he was traveling on the road to Damascus to persecute more Christians. On his way, the Bible says suddenly a light from heaven shined on Saul. The light was so bright, it blinded Saul. He fell to the ground and the voice spoke to Saul, "Saul, Saul, why do you persecute me?" Saul knew it was God. He replied, "Who are you, Lord?" God said, "I am Jesus, whom you are persecuting." The Bible tells us that God changed Saul's name to Paul and Paul became a powerful witness and instrumental in building the kingdom of God. (Acts 9:1-9)

We all must have a conversion experience. You can't be effective in ministry without it. This experience causes you to seek God's will in all matters and devote yourselves to the love of God and service to your neighbor by utilizing the gifts and callings. The most important discovery you can make is who you are in God and your divine purpose. God is our creator. It is important to learn why we were created, keeping in mind we were created for God's purpose and to be involved in God's plan through the ministry of Jesus Christ. The Bible says Jesus ascended high in the heavens and has given every grace and a gift. Let's search the scriptures and make sure we have accepted the foundational calls.

Ephesians 4:7-8 **But unto every one of us is given grace according to the measure of the gift of Christ. Wherefore he saith, When He ascended up on high, He led captivity captive, and gave gifts unto men.**

Why is grace important? _____

_____

_____

_____

_____

_____

_____

_____

_____

Now that scripture confirms that everyone has a gift, this course was developed to assure you of what that gift is. It is dangerous to claim a gift that God hasn't called you to do. God can't empower you or protect you when you operate against His will. God's claims us as his. It should be comforting to know that we all were created and designed for Him.

***Psalm 100:3* Know ye that the Lord He is God: It is He that hath made us, and not we ourselves; we are His people and the sheep of His pasture.**

Why is knowing who made you is important to your walk with God? _____

_____

_____

_____

_____

_____

There is nothing mysterious about hearing the call from God. Scripture tells us that when God calls, we know that it is a call from God. The call comes to those God draws.

John 6:44-51 **No man can come to me, except the Father which hath sent me draw him; and I will raise him up at the last day. It is written in the prophets, And they shall be all taught of God. Every man therefore that hath heard, and hath learned of the Father, cometh unto Me.**

John 10:27-28 **My sheep hear my voice, and I know them, and they follow Me: And I give unto them eternal life; and they shall never perish, neither shall any man pluck them out of my hand.**

Why is it important to know the voice of God?_____

_____

_____

_____

_____

_____

_____

Everything is based upon being reconciled with Jesus. There are 3 calls that you must respond to no longer be alienated from the presence of God. In addition, these 3 calls are the foundation of knowing who you are and having the assurance to know that God anointed you for every position. A relationship with Jesus Christ allows

God to empower you for the work of the ministry. The first call is the call to salvation, the second call is the call to holiness, and the third call is the call to service. Let's see what the Bible says about these foundational calls.

First call: Call to Salvation

Acts 2:38 **Then Peter said unto them, Repent, and be baptized every one of you in the name of Jesus Christ for the remission of sins, and ye shall receive the gift of the Holy Spirit.**

Romans 10:9-10 **That if thou confess with thy mouth the Lord Jesus, and shalt believe in thine heart that God hath raised Him from the dead, thou shalt be saved. For with the heart man believeth unto righteousness; and with the mouth confession is made unto salvation.**

When you accept the call to salvation, you are reconciled to Christ, and we are sanctified through the blood of Jesus Christ. Without the shedding of blood, there is no forgiveness of sins.

Matthew 26:28 **For this is my blood of the new testament, which is shed for many for the remission of sins.**

Hebrews 9:22 **And almost all things are by the law purged with blood; and without shedding of blood is no remission.**

Hebrews 13:12 **Wherefore Jesus also, that He might sanctify the people with His own blood, suffered without the gate.**

How has the blood of the New Testament change your life? _____

_____

_____

_____

_____

_____

_____

_____

When you respond to the call of salvation not only activate the blood of Jesus in your life, but you welcome God's Spirit (The Holy Spirit) to manifest into your life. We are sealed with God when the Holy Spirit comes alive in the believer.

Ezekiel 36:27 **And I will put my spirit within you, and cause you to walk in My statutes, and ye shall keep my judgments, and do them.**

I Corinthians 3:16 **Know ye not that ye are the temple of God, and the at the Spirit of God dwelleth in you?**

Ephesians 4:30 **And grieve not the Holy Spirit of God, whereby ye are sealed unto the day of redemption.**

Why do you need God's Spirit to live in you? _____

_____

_____

_____

_____

_____

_____

_____

Since we have accepted the call of salvation, activated the blood of Jesus in our lives, and have become sealed with God, we must say YES to the 2nd call, the call to holiness.

Second call: Call to Holiness

Many believers accept the call to salvation and attempt to skip over the call to holiness and call directly to the next call of service. The problem is anyone who doesn't accept the call to holiness can't be effective. There are many things that we have to lay aside when we come to Jesus to be empowered for service. You are not going to be anointed by God holding onto how we use to do things, because the Bible tells us we are a new creature. The call may be heard, but you have to accept and consent to the call to allow things to become new.

2 Corinthians 5:17 **Therefore if any man be in Christ, he is a new creature; old things are passed away; behold, all things are become new.**

II Timothy **Who hath saved us, and called us with an holy calling, not according to our works, but according to His own purpose and grace, which was given us in Christ Jesus before the world began.**

Why is holiness important to the call? _____

_____

_____

_____

_____

_____

_____

_____

We are searching the scriptures to confirm that God, Himself called us to be holy. There is no compromising, and you can't ignore this call. To be holy is not to be perfect, but to be dedicated to God and your actions reflect the character of God. The call of holiness gives you a spirit of conviction. This conviction causes you to quickly repent for wrongful deeds, actions, reactions, and thoughts. Let's hear the call of holiness.

I Peter 5:15-16 **But as He hath called you is holy, so be ye holy in all manner of conversation; Because it is written, Be ye holy; for I am holy.**

How has holiness changed your life? _____

_____

_____

_____

_____

_____

_____

_____

The Bible gives us clear instructions on how to accept the call to holiness.

Hebrews 12:1 **Wherefore seeing we also are compassed about with so great a cloud of witnesses, let us lay aside every weight, and the sin which doth so easily beset us, and let us run with patience the race that is set before us.**

Romans 13:14 **But put ye on the Lord Jesus Christ, and make not provision for the flesh, to fulfill the lusts thereof.**

I Peter 1:14 **As obedient children, not fashioning yourselves according to the former lusts in our ignorance:**

Ephesians 1:4 **According as He hath chosen us in Him before the foundation of the world, that we should be holy and without blame before Him in love;**

What is the power behind getting your flesh disciplined? _____

_____

_____

_____

_____

_____

The 3rd call comes when you have given God an eternal YES to the first two calls. Yes, to the call of salvation, yes to the call of holiness, and now you are ready to say yes to the call of service. We are called to serve. Service means we are committed to serving others and using our lives to serve many.

Third call: Call to Service

God promises to empower those whom he calls. Accepting the call when called, God equips His servants for the mission. The moment you say Yes to God, you are submitting to God's will and God's ways. We are then ready for service.

Psalm 90:17 **And let the beauty of the Lord our God be upon us; and establish thou the work of our hands upon us; yea, the work of our hands establish it.**

I Peter 4:10 **As every man hath received the gift, even so minister the same one to another, as good stewards of manifold grace of God.**

Mark 10:45 **For even the Son of man came not to be ministered unto, but to minister, and to give His life a ransom for many.**

Colossians 3:23 **And whatsoever ye do, do it heartily, as to the Lord, and not unto men;**

How do you know you are ready for the call to service? _____

_____

_____

_____

_____

_____

_____

CHAPTER 2
HOMEWORK

1. What is the first call? _____

   Have you received the first call? _____ Yes _____ No

   Are you willing to let go of all and any unforgiveness? _____ Yes _____ No

Do you remember what occurred when you received the first call? _____

_____

_____

_____

_____

_____

_____

2. What is the second call? _____

   Have you received the second call? _____ Yes _____ No

   Are you willing to let go of all and any unforgiveness? _____ Yes _____ No

Do you remember what occurred when you received the second call? _____

_____

_____

_____

_____

_____

_____

3.   What is the third call? _____

       Have you received the third call?   _____ Yes   _____ No

Do you remember what occurred when you received the third call? _____

_____

_____

_____

_____

_____

_____

Read about the Apostle Paul's conversion experience, Acts 9:1-9. Tell us about your conversion experience. Please include how as a result of this experience how has your life changed? Does this experience excite you to help others? If yes, in what ways? Please write one to two pages.

CHAPTER 3

Knowing Who You Are In God

Now that you have responded to the 3 foundational calls, it is now time to know without any doubts about the gifts and callings that operate in your life. It all begins with getting to know who you are in God and to God.

It is believed that in order to know who you are in God, you must first know who God is. In Matthew 16:13-19, Jesus came into the coast of Caesarea Philippi. He asked His disciples a question, "Whom do men say that I the Son of man am?" The Bible say they told Jesus who the people were identifying Him to be. They replied that some thought He was John the Baptist, some said He was Elias, others stated Jesus was Jeremiah, and those who were not sure called Him one of the prophets. Then Jesus asked a critical question, "But whom say ye that I am?" The Bible says that Simon Peter answered and said, "Thou are the Christ, the Son of the living God." Scripture doesn't state whether Jesus was shocked or proud, but he says, Jesus answered, "Blessed art thou, Simon Barjona: for flesh and blood hath not revealed it unto thee, but my Father which is in heaven. And I say unto thee, That thou art Peter, and upon this rock I will build my church; and the gates of hell shall not prevail against it. And I will give unto thee the keys of the kingdom of heaven; and whatsoever thou shalt bind on earth shall be bound in heaven; and whatsoever thou shalt loose on earth shall be loosed in heaven."

When you study Peter's life, you will learn that he acknowledged Jesus as the Son of God and God used him to do great things. In Acts 2:41 you read how Peter ministered God's Word and those that received the word was baptized. The Bible tells us in one day, under the ministry that God gave Peter, three thousand souls were added to the church. We have to know who God is and then we can identify who we are in Him.

Gifts and callings come directly from God and God gives spiritual gifts to help those who answer the call to be impactful, effective, and influential in the lives of God's people. People can have or operate in several gifts. Some may be recognizable while others may not be as dominant. Knowing your spiritual self is important. When you make that discovery, you can walk in the confidence of God.

When people are willing to uncover their most intimate, inner subjective part of who they are, they grow in the presence of God. The spiritual self is the inner essence of who you are to God and your purpose for this world. Knowing who you are is essential for understanding your identity and being effective in the ministry that God created you to do. Although you have been called or you have various gifts, doesn't mean that you are effective. You must understand that gifts and calls are without repentance. God tells us about His gifts and callings that He graciously has given His people.

Romans 11:29 **For the gifts and calling of God are without repentance.**

Without repentance means that whatever you were created to do or gifted to do, God does not take it away. The effectiveness of that gift and calling is based upon your obedience through your relationship with Jesus Christ. However, you still have it, but just how you want to operate in that call, and gift is up to you.

People who want to be seen can't be effective because it is all about them. People who want God to be seen through them is effective. Why? Because it is all about God and not about them. Therefore, they are not trying to share in God's glory. Remember when Moses entered into the presence of God? Not only did he receive the Ten Commandments, God also, let him know what he expected from every one of His people.

Exodus 34:14 **For thou shalt worship no other god; for the Lord, whose name is Jealous, is a jealous God.**

How as identifying with who you are in God changed your life?_____

_____

_____

_____

_____

_____

_____

You can be an eloquent speaker, have a charismatic personality, or even just be a likable person. They are good qualities, but they don't make you effective. It is the anointing of the Holy Spirit that makes you effective. The anointing of God takes sacrifice, denying oneself, holiness, loneliness, and obedience. Let me repeat, to be effective you to be anointed by God. Let's read what God says about His anointing (power):

Zechariah 4:6b …. **Not by might, nor by power, but by my spirit, saith the Lord of hosts.**

I John 2:27 **But the anointing which ye have received of Him abideth in you, and ye need not that any man teach you; but as the same anointing teacheth you of all things, and is truth, and is no lie, and even as it hath taught you, ye shall abide in him.**

Isaiah 61:1-11 **The Spirit of the Lord God is upon me; because the Lord hath anointed me to preach good tidings unto the meek; he hath sent me to bind up the brokenhearted, to proclaim liberty to the captives, and the opening of the prison to them that are bound.**

Luke 4:18 **The Spirit of the Lord is upon me, because He hath anointed me to preach the gospel to the poor; He hath sent me to heal the brokenhearted, to preach deliverance to the captives, and recovering of sight to the blind, to set at liberty them that are bruised,**

How are these scriptures applied to your life? _____

_____

_____

_____

_____

_____

Now that we have established based upon the word of God what is needed to be effective in ministry, let's now evaluate who we are.

Who Am I?

To have the assurance of your calling you need to know who you are. What are your weaknesses? What are your strengths? What areas can you improve? All of these questions are answered by getting to know who you are and being truthful to yourself. Then you can make your calling and election sure. The Bible addresses the issue of thinking you know who you are.

Galatians 6:3-5 **For if a man think himself to be something, when he is nothing, he deceiveth himself. But let every man prove his own work, and then shall he have rejoicing in him alone, and not in another. For every man shall bear his own burden.**

Do you know who you are in God? If so, tell us. _____

_____

_____

_____

_____

_____

_____

It is in the presence of God you will be shown your true inner self. God knows us better than we know ourselves. When Jeremiah received the call from God, he told us what happened in the first chapter of Jeremiah. There are many scriptures where God informs us just who we are. Let's look at a few of them.

Jeremiah 1:4-5 **Then the word of the Lord came unto me saying, Before I formed thee in the belly I knew thee; and before thou camest forth out of the womb I sanctified thee, and I ordained thee a prophet unto the nations.**

Psalm 100:3 **Know ye that the Lord He is God: it is He that hath made us, and not we ourselves; we are His people, and the sheep of His pasture.**

Psalm 139:14 **I will praise thee; for I am fearfully and wonderfully made: marvellous are thy works; and that my soul knoweth right well.**

I Peter 2:9 **But ye are a chosen generation, a royal priesthood, an holy nation, a peculiar people; that ye should shew forth the praises of Him who hath called you out of darkness into His marvellous light;**

How do you feel now that you know who you are? _____

_____

_____

_____

_____

_____

For God to reveal who you are this requires you to stay in the presence of God. We must keep in mind, that God knows who we are, and we must get to know who we are in God. That is how you make your calling and election sure.

Psalm 139:1-3, **O lord, thou hast searched me, and known me. Thou knowest my downsitting and mine uprising, thou understandest my thoughts afar off. Thou compassest my path and my lying down, and art acquainted with all my ways.**

II Peter 1:10-11 **Wherefore the rather, brethren give diligence to make your calling and election sure: for so an entrance shall be ministered unto you abundantly into the everlasting kingdom of our Lord and Saviour Jesus Christ.**

What is your understanding of how God sees you? _____

_____

_____

_____

_____

_____

_____

For homework, you will be asked to do a thorough self-evaluation. We will discuss your revelation in the next class.

HOMEWORK

Tell us who you are. _____

_____

_____

_____

_____

_____

What do people say about you? . _____

_____

_____

_____

_____

What ministries are you currently working in? _____

_____

_____

_____

_____

_____

Which ministries did you enjoy, and which ministries were hard for you? _____

_____

_____

_____

_____

_____

What do you expect to get from this class? _____

_____

_____

_____

_____

_____

_____

Read Matthew 16:13-19 and tell us about the day you came into the true knowledge of who God was and how did it change your life. Write one to two pages.

What Does God Say About You?

In the Book of Romans 16:16, the Apostle Paul reveals something to the church by the leading of the Holy Spirit. He said, "Let not your good be evil spoken of." Once you discover who God is, and who you are in God, you have a responsibility to God and His people. Carelessness, being prideful, controlling, and selfish can damage your Gospel message and lead to people turning from God instead of to God. That is more damaging than marring your reputation. A weaken the message and makes you ineffective.

In Luke 13:6-9, Jesus spoke the parable of the fig tree. The Bible says Jesus told how a certain man had planted a fig tree in his vineyard. He continued to expect to receive fruit from the tree, but there was none. The man inquired why for three years he came seeking fruit from the tree and each time there was no fruit. He instructed the dresser of the vineyard to cut the tree down to the ground. The dresser of the vineyard pleaded for the tree and asked the owner of the vineyard to give the tree one more year to bear fruit. The man agreed and said that if there is no fruit on the tree in a year it will definitely be cut down. People that don't bring forth fruit is just like the fig tree, doomed to be cut down.

The Apostle Paul goes on to remind us in this letter, Romans 16:17-19, "For the kingdom of God is not meat and drink; but righteousness, and peace, and joy in the Holy Ghost. For he that in these things serveth Christ is acceptable to God, and approved of men. Let us therefore follow after the things which make for peace, and things wherewith one may edify another." Let's search the scriptures and see how God sees His people.

Light to the World

Matthew 5:14-16 **You are the light of the world. A city set on a hill cannot be hidden. Neither do men light a candle, and put it under a bushel, but on a candlestick; and it giveth light unto all that are in the house. Let your light so shine before men, that they may see your good works, and glorify your Father which is in heaven.**

Philippians 2:15-16 **…That you may be blameless and harmless, the sons of God, without rebuke, in the midst of a crooked and perverse nation, among whom ye shine as lights in the world; holding forth the word of life; that I may rejoice in the day of Christ, that I have not run in vain, neither laboured in vain.**

2 Corinthians 4:6 **For God, who commanded the light to shine out of darkness, hath shined in our hearts, to give the light of the knowledge of the glory of God in the face of Jesus Christ.**

1 Thessalonians 5:5 **Ye are all the children of light, and the children of the day: we are not of the night, nor of darkness.**

How has the knowledge of you being a light changed your perspective of yourself? _____

_____

_____

_____

_____

_____

Called into the Family of God

Hebrews 3:1 **Wherefore, holy brethren, partakers of the heavenly calling, consider the Apostle and High Priest of our profession, Christ Jesus;**

1 Corinthians 12:27 **Now ye are the body of Christ, and members in particular.**

Have you applied these scriptures to your life? If so, what has changed. _____

_____

_____

_____

_____

You Have Went from Victim to Victor

Romans 8:37 Nay, in all these things we are more than conquerors through Him that loved us.

1 John 5:4-5 For whatsoever is born of God overcometh the world: and this is the victory that overcometh the world, even our faith. Who is he that overcometh the world, but he that believeth that Jesus is the Son of God?

What have you conquerored? _____

_____

_____

_____

_____

_____

You Are a Children and Heirs with God

John 1:12-13 But as many as received Him, to them gave He power to become the sons of God, even to them that believe on His name. Which were born, not of blood, nor of the will of the flesh, nor the will of man, but of God.

Galatians 3:26-28 For ye are the children of God by faith in Christ Jesus. For as many of you as have been baptized into Christ have put on Christ. There is neither Jew nor Greek, there is neither bond nor free, there is neither male nor female: for ye are all one in Christ Jesus.

Romans 8:16-17 The Spirit itself beareth witness with our spirit, that we are the children of God: and if children, then heirs; heirs of God, and joint-heirs with Christ: if so be that we suffer with Him, that we may be also glorified together.

How has the power of God changed your lifestyle? _____

_____

_____

_____

_____

_____

_____

You Are Chosen By God

1 Peter 2:9 But ye are a chosen generation, a royal priesthood, an holy nation, a peculiar people; that ye should shew forth the praises of Him who hath called you out of darkness into His marvellous light;

John 15:16 Ye have not chosen me, but I have chosen you, and ordained you, that ye should go and bring forth fruit, and that your fruit should remain; that whatsoever ye shall ask of the Father in my name, He may give it you.

Jeremiah 1:5 Before I formed thee in the belly I knew thee; and before thou camest forth out of the womb I sanctified thee, and I ordained thee a prophet unto the nations.

How do you know God chose you? _____

_____

_____

_____

_____

_____

God called You A New Creation and A Friend

2 Corinthians 5:17 Therefore if any man be in Christ, he is a new creation; old things are passed away; behold all things are become new.

John 15:15 Henceforth, I call you not servants; for the servant knoweth not what his lord doeth: but I called you friends; for all the things that I have heard of my Father I have made known unto you.

Galatians 2:20 I am crucified with Christ: nevertheless I live; yet not I, but Christ liveth in me: and the life which I now live in the flesh I live by the faith of the Son of God, who loved me, and gave Himself for me.

Colossians 3:3 For ye are dead, and your life is hid with Christ in God.

In what way have servanthood impacted your life? _____

_____

_____

_____

_____

_____

_____

You Are Called to be Saints

Corinthians 1:2 Unto the church of God which is at Corinth, to them that are sanctified in Christ Jesus, called to be saints, with all that in every place call upon the name of Jesus Christ our Lord, both their's and our's.

Ephesians 2:19 Now therefore ye are no more strangers and foreigners, but fellowcitizens with the saints, and the household of God.

Colossians 1:26 Even the mystery which hath been hid from ages and from generations, but now is made manifest to His saints.

How do you know you are sanctified?

_____

_____

_____

_____

_____

You Are the Salt of the Earth

Matthew 5:13 Ye are the salt of the earth: but if the salt have lost his savour, wherewith shall it be salted? It is thenceforth good for nothing, but to cast out, and to be trodden under foot of men.

How are you using your position to impact the lives of others?

_____

_____

_____

_____

You Are the Temple of God

1 Corinthians 3:16 Know ye not that ye are the temple of God, and that the Spirit of God dwelleth in you?

1 Corinthians 6:19-20 What? Know ye not that your body is the temple of the Holy Ghost which is in you, which ye have of God, and ye are not your own? For ye are bought with a price: therefore glorify God in your body, and in your spirit, which are God's.

How have you applied these scriptures to your life? _____

_____

_____

_____

_____

HOMEWORK

There are many more scriptures that God helps you to know who you are in Him when you receive your call. Locate two additional scriptures that tell you who you are to God:

1) Scripture: _____

_____

_____

_____

_____

2) Scripture: _____

_____

_____

_____

_____

You heard the call, you accepted the call, and you know who you are in God's eyesight. Here are some questions to ask yourself:

1.	Are you willing to handle the call with care?	_____ Yes	_____ No
2.	Are you willing to be responsible with the call?	_____ Yes	_____ No
3.	Are you ready for the call to service?	_____ Yes	_____ No
4.	Do you know who you are to God?	_____ Yes	_____ No
5.	Will you be a light?	_____ Yes	_____ No
6.	Are you displaying the image of Christ?	_____ Yes	_____ No

Write a one to two page paper and telling us how God sees you.

Requirements To Be Effective In Gifts And Callings

The story of Abraham starts in Genesis 11:27-25:11. It covers a great deal of the Book of Genesis. Abraham is regarded as a major patriarch of Christianity. Abraham had a relationship with God. In Genesis 12, God told Abraham to get out of his father's house, out of his country and He would lead him to a land that He would show him. As a result of his obedience, God promised Abraham, I will make you a great nation, I will bless you, your name would be great, and you will be a blessing to many. Abraham's requirement was to be obedient to God and leave what was familiar to him, to depart from his earthly father's protection and rely on His heavenly Father's protection, and trust in God.

Many may ask, what does the gift and call require me to do? If you read Abraham's story, you will find it costs you everything that you perceive to be valuable. Remember God does not call the equipped, God anoints the called. Now let's look at what God requires us to do once we respond to the call.

Put on The Whole Armor of God

Ephesians 6:11-13 **Put on the whole armor of God, that ye may be able to stand against the wiles of the devil. For we wrestle not against flesh and blood, but against principalities, against powers, against the rulers of the darkness of this world, against spiritual wickedness in high places. Wherefore take unto you the whole armor of God, that ye may be able to withstand in the evil day, and having done all, to stand.**

Is there any part of the armor of God that needs to be replaced in your life? _____

_____

_____

_____

_____

God Is Your Confidence

Proverbs 3:26 **For the Lord shall be thy confidence, and shall keep thy foot from being taken.**

How as the confidence of God impact your life of service? _____

_____

_____

_____

_____

_____

Walk Worthy of the Vocation Which You Are Called

Ephesians 4:1-2 **I therefore, the prisoner of the Lord, beseech you that you walk worthy of the vocation wherewith ye are called, with all lowliness and meekness, with longsuffering, forbearing one another in love.**

How do you know you are walking worth of the vocation in which you were called? _____

_____

_____

_____

_____

Have Need of Patience

Hebrews 10:36 **For ye have need of patience, that, after ye have done the will of God, ye might receive the promise.**

Why do you feel we need patience? _____

_____

_____

_____

_____

_____

You Need Faith

Hebrews 11:1-2 Now faith is the substance of things hoped for, the evidence of things not seen. For by it the elders obtained a good report.

Hebrews 11:6 But without faith it is impossible to please Him; for he that cometh to God must believe that He is, and that He is a rewarder of them that diligently seek Him.

Why is faith so important in your life? _____

_____

_____

_____

_____

Present Your Bodies as a Living Sacrifice and Be Transformed

Romans 12:1-2 I beseech you therefore, brethren, by the mercies of God, that ye present your bodies a living sacrifice, holy, acceptable unto God, which is your reasonable service. And be not conformed to this world, but be ye transformed by the renewing of your mind, that ye may prove what is that good, and acceptable, and perfect, will of God.

Have you applied this scripture to your life? If so, how has your life changed? _____

_____

_____

_____

_____

The Word of God Must Dwell In You

Colossians 3:16 Let the word of Christ dwell in you richly in all wisdom; teaching and admonishing one another in psalms and hymns and spiritual songs, singing with grace in your hearts to the Lord.

2 Timothy 2:15 Study to shew thyself approved unto God, a workman that needeth not to be ashamed, rightly dividing the word of truth.

Why is the knowledge of God important in your life? _____

_____

_____

_____

Endure Hardness and Be A Soldier

2 Timothy 2:3 Thou therefore endure hardness, as a good soldier of Jesus Christ.

Why is the knowledge of God important in your life? _____

_____

_____

Deny Yourself and Be Willing to Suffer

2 Timothy 2:11-12 It is a faithful saying, for if we be dead with Him, we shall also live with Him. If we suffer, we shall also reign with Him, if we deny Him, he also will deny us.

Luke 9:23 And He said to them all, if any man will come after me, let him deny himself, and take up his cross, and follow me.

In what ways do you deny yourself to follow Jesus? _____

_____

_____

_____

You Have To Pray and Fast

Philippians 4:5-6 Let your moderation be known unto all men, The Lord is at hand. Be careful for nothing; but in every thing by prayer and supplication with thanksgiving let your requests be made know unto God.

1 Thessalonians 5:17-18 Pray without ceasing. In every thing give thanks: for this is the will of God in Christ Jesus concerning you.

Proverbs 8:17 I love them that love Me; and those that seek me early shall find Me.

Jeremiah 29:12-13 Then shall ye all upon Me, and ye shall go and pray unto Me, and I will hearken unto you. And ye shall seek me, and find me, when ye shall search for me with all your heart.

Lamentations 3:25 The Lord is good unto them that wait for Him, to the soul that seeketh Him.

Why is seeking God vital to your walk with God? _____

_____

HOMEWORK

Name the requirements to be effective:

1. _____

2. _____

3. _____

4. _____

5. _____

6. _____

7. _____

8. _____

9. _____

10. _____

11. List any other requirements that may not have been listed:

_____

_____

_____

_____

_____

12. Are there any of the requirements you feel you lack? _____ Yes _____ No

13. Which requirement do you feel you lack and why? _____

_____

_____

_____

_____

14. What are you doing to be strengthened in all of the requirements? _____

_____

_____

_____

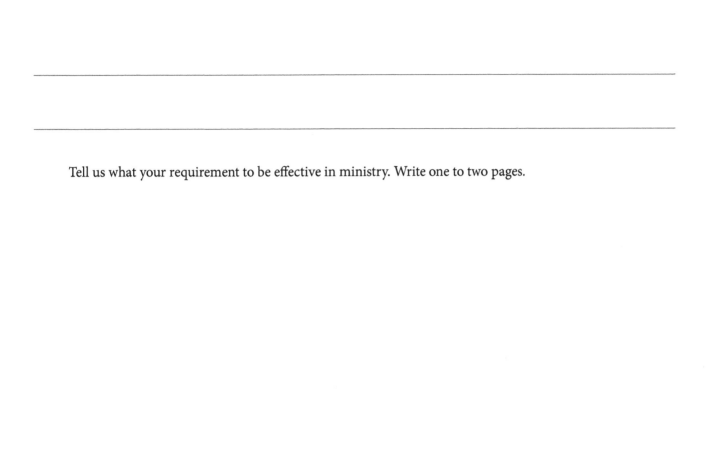

Tell us what your requirement to be effective in ministry. Write one to two pages.

Identifying Your Leadership Calls

Moses is one of the key figures in the history of Christianity. The story of Moses begins with a boy born into the tribe of Levi. He was born a slave. Moses was born at a time when the number of Israelites were growing immensely, and it caused Pharaoh to fear that the Israelites would overpower the Egyptians. Pharaoh ordered all male infants to be drowned in the Nile River to avoid an uprising. Moses' mother didn't want him to die and placed him in a basket and put him on the river. The Bible lets us know that Pharaoh's daughter heard Moses crying in the basket. She had her maid draw him out of the water. Pharaoh's daughter raised Moses as her son.

Moses grew up as an Egyptian. When Moses got older, he had compassion for the Israelites and recognized how bad they were being treated. When Moses noticed an Egyptian slaver beating an Israelite, he killed the Egyptian and hid the body. Mose fled Egypt and went to Midian. The Bible tells us that Moses met his wife in Midian. It was during Moses' time in Midian that he had an encounter with the true and living God. It was through this encounter that God gave Moses instructions on how he was going to return to Egypt and lead the Israelites to a land that He has for them. When you read Exodus, you read how God proved Himself to be God.

Just like Moses, leaders need an encounter with God. Leadership requires instruction and direction from the Lord of Lord and Kings of King. Success in leadership requires leaders to follow God. Exodus 33:11-16

Scripture lists many gifts that God has distributed throughout the body of Christ. Let's read what the scripture says about gifts.

1 Corinthians 12:4-7 **Now there are diversities of gifts, but the same Spirit and there are differences of administration, but the same Lord and there are diversities of operations, but it is the same God which worketh all in all. But the manifestation of the Spirit is given to every man to profit withal.**

1 Corinthians 12:28 **God hath set some in the church, first apostles, secondarily prophets, thirdly teachers, after then miracles, then gifts of healings, helps, governments, diversities**

1 Corinthians 12:4-7 **Now there are diversities of gifts, but the same Spirit and there are differences of administration, but the same Lord and there are diversities of operations, but it is the same God which worketh all in all. But the manifestation of the Spirit is given to every man to profit withal.**

Ephesians 4:11-12. **And he gave some, apostles; and some, prophets; and some, evangelists; and some pastors and teachers; For the perfecting of the saints, for the work of the ministry, for the edifying of the body of Christ.**

1 Corinthians 12:28 **God hath set some in the church, first apostles, secondarily prophets, thirdly teachers, after then miracles, then gifts of healings, helps, governments, diversities**

APOSTLES – The term *apostle* means "one who is sent." Technically, however, an apostle was more than a messenger. The chief apostle in the New Testament is Jesus Himself. He was sent by the Father and spoke with the authority invested in Him by the Father. The role of the Apostle is a call to plant and oversee churches and to mentor believers in the ministry of Jesus Christ.

Are you called to the office of an Apostle? _____ Yes _____ No

PROPHETS – The role of the prophet in the life of God's people is to serve as a spokesperson or meditator for God. Prophets receive direction from God on how to help God's people and help navigate challenges and situations in life. The gift of prophecy is the special ability that certain members of the Body of Christ must receive and communicate messages from God to His people through a divine anointed utterance.

Are you called to the office of the Prophet?_____ Yes _____ No

EVANGELISTS – Evangelists are often known for their powerful preaching and public speaking abilities. They may preach in a variety of settings, such as churches, outdoor events, or revival meetings. The evangelist's primary role is the share the good news of Jesus Christ with others.

Are you called to the office of the Evangelist? _____ Yes _____ No

PASTORS – A pastor provides leadership to members of the church and guides the church community. They are responsible for shepherding the flock, teaching and preaching the Word of God, providing spiritual guidance, and caring for the needs of the congregation. This calling is essential. Pastors are called by God, chosen, and appointed to serve and lead God's people.

Are you called to the office of the Pastor? _____ Yes _____ No

TEACHERS – A teacher can impart the truth and wisdom of Jesus Christ. The role of a teacher in the church is to help others grow in their faith, develop a deeper understanding of the Bible and Christian principles, and live out the teachings of Jesus Christ in their daily lives.

Are you called to the office of the Teacher? _____ Yes _____ No

OFFICE OF A BISHOP: A bishop is an overseer of the church. This office is responsible for appointing and supervising other leaders and ensuring the upholding of the doctrine of the Bible. Bishop is mentioned 6 times in the Bible in 1 Timothy, Titus, and Philippians.

Are you called to the office of a bishop?_____ Yes _____ No

HOMEWORK

1. Has God called you to any leadership roles? _____ Yes _____ No

If yes, what are your current leadership roles? _____

_____

_____

_____

_____

_____

2. Are there any leadership roles you are called to but not currently serving in? _____ Yes _____ No

If yes, what are they? _____

_____

_____

_____

3. Are you involved in any leadership roles that God has not called you to? _____ Yes _____ No

If yes, let us know what roles that is? _____

_____

_____

_____

_____

_____

_____

Read Exodus 33. Tell us if you ever experienced an encounter with God. Write one to two pages and let us know what happened. How did it change your life?

Identifying Your Spiritual Gifts

You don't have to have just one gift. You could have multiple gifts. Some are more dominant than others. Let's identify your gifts. Read the definition of each gift and check when you have the gift, don't have the gift, or you are not sure.

ADMINISTRATION: The ability to help steer the church, or a ministry, toward the successful completion of God-given goals, with skills in planning, organization, and supervision.

Have you been gifted in administration? _____ Yes _____ No _____Unsure

DISCERNMENT: The wisdom to recognize truth from untruth by correctly evaluating whether a behavior or teaching is from God or another, ungodly source.

Do you have the gift of discernment? _____ Yes _____ No _____Unsure

EVANGELISM: The ability to successfully communicate the message of the gospel, especially to nonbelievers. You can be gifted for evangelism and not be called to the office of an evangelist.

Do you have the gift of evangelism? _____ Yes _____ No _____Unsure

EXHORTATION: Competence in offering encouragement, comfort, and support to help someone be all that God wants them to be.

Are you gifted with exhortation? _____ Yes _____ No _____Unsure

FAITH: People with this gift have such great confidence in the power and promises of God that they can stand strong in their belief, no matter what may try to shake them. They can also stand up for the church and for their faith in such a way as to defend and move it forward. Every man is given a measure of faith.

Are you gifted with a huge amount of faith? _____ Yes _____ No _____Unsure

GIVING: Those who have this gift are particularly willing and able to share what resources they have with pleasure and without the need to see them returned.

Is giving one of the spiritual gifts? _____ Yes _____ No _____Unsure

HEALING: A capability used by God to restore others, be that physically, emotionally, mentally, or spiritually.

Is healing one of your spiritual gifts?_____ Yes _____ No _____Unsure

HELPS: Someone with this gift can support or assist members of the body of Christ so that they may be free to minister to others.

Do you have the gift of helps? _____ Yes _____ No _____Unsure

HOSPITALITY: A natural ability to make people—even strangers—feel welcome in one's own home or church to disciple or serve them

Are you gifted with hospitality? _____ Yes _____ No _____Unsure

KNOWLEDGE: This is the gift of someone who actively pursues knowledge of the Bible. This person may also enjoy analyzing biblical data.

Is knowledge one of your spiritual gifts? _____ Yes _____ No _____Unsure

LEADERSHIP: This aptitude marks a person who can stand before a church, direct the body with care and attention, and motivate them toward achieving the church's goals.

Is leadership one of your spiritual gifts? _____ Yes _____ No _____Unsure

MERCY: This is the defining trait of a person with great sensitivity for those who are suffering. It manifests itself in offering compassion and encouragement, and in a love for giving practical help to someone in need.

Is mercy one of your spiritual gifts? _____ Yes _____ No _____Unsure

PROPHECY: The ability to speak the message of God to others. This sometimes involves foresight or visions of what is to come. This skill should be used only to offer encouragement or warning. You can have the gift of prophecy and not be called to the office of the prophet.

Do you have the gift of prophecy? _____ Yes _____ No _____Unsure

SERVING: A talent for identifying tasks needed for the body of Christ and using available resources to get the job done.

SPEAKING IN TONGUES: The supernatural ability to speak in another language (one that has not been learned).

Do you have the gift of speaking in unknown tongues? _____ Yes _____ No _____Unsure

INTERPRETATION OF UNKNOWN TONGUES: Those who have the interpretation of tongues can share with the listeners that heavenly message that is shared in an unknown language. Read 1 Corinthians 14:26-28

Do you have the gift of interpreting unknown tongues? _____ Yes _____ No _____Unsure

TEACHING: The skill to teach from the Bible and communicate it effectively for the understanding and spiritual growth of others. You can have the gift to teach and not be called to the office of the teacher.

Do you have the gift of teaching? _____ Yes _____ No _____Unsure

WISDOM: The gift of being able to sort through facts and data to discover what needs to be done for the church.

Is the word of wisdom one of your gifts? _____ Yes _____ No _____Unsure

WORKING OF MIRACLES: The working of miracles is a manifestation of God's power that is not limited to physical healing. Miracles are a supernatural occurrence that goes beyond our human scope of comprehension. When someone is gifted with the gift of miracles that have the power of the Holy Spirit to bend the natural laws of the world.

Are you gifted with the working of miracles? _____ Yes _____ No _____Unsure

CHAPTER 7
HOMEWORK

List every gift that you are confident you have and tell us how you received the gift or how you know you have the gift.

1) Gift/Calling _____

How did you receive the call? _____

_____

_____

_____

_____

2) Gift/Calling _____

How did you receive the call? _____

_____

_____

_____

3) Gift/Calling _____

How did you receive the call? _____

_____

_____

_____

_____

4) Gift/Calling _____

How did you receive the call? _____

_____

_____

_____

5) Gift/Calling _____

How did you receive the call? _____

_____

_____

_____

_____

6) Gift/Calling _____

How did you receive the call? _____

_____

_____

_____

7) Gift/Calling _____

How did you receive the call? _____

_____

_____

_____

8) Gift/Calling _____

How did you receive the call? _____

_____

_____

_____

_____

9) Gift/Calling _____

How did you receive the call? _____

_____

_____

_____

10) Gift/Calling _____

How did you receive the call? _____

_____

_____

_____

CHAPTER 8

Confirmation Of The Call

In the Book of Matthew 25:14-30, you read the parable of the talents. The Bible says that a man travelling into a far country called his servants and gave them talents according to their ability. One servant received five talents, another servant received two talents and another one talent. The servant with the five talents he went and traded them. The servant with two talents gained another two talents. The servant with the one talent buried his talent. The servants that used their talents, his lord said unto them, "well done, thou good and faithful servant: thou hast been faithful over a few things, I will make thee ruler over many things; enter thou into the joy of the lord." The servant that hid his talent due to fear, his lord said unto him, "Thou wicked and slothful servant, thou knewest that I reap where I sowed not, and gather where I have not strawed: Thou oughtest therefore tohave put my money to the exchangers, and then at my coming I should have received mine own usury. Take therefore the talent from him, and give it unto him which hath ten talents." The Bible says the unprofitable servant was cast into outer darkness where there was weeping and gnashing of teeth.

The message for every person who has identified what their gifts and callings you now have the responsibility to use them for the glory of God. If you don't use them, you will be like the servant with one talent. It will be taken from you, and you will be cast into outer darkness.

In the last chapter you examined your calls and gifts, then you identified your gifts or calls. Now that you are confirming those gifts and callings that is operating in your life, you are obligated to use them to glorify God.

1) Were there any gifts/callings that you are now second-guessing? _____Yes _____ No

If so, what are they and why are you second-guessing? _____

_____

_____

_____

2) Were there any gifts/callings that you are now second-guessing? _____Yes _____ No

If so, what are they and why are you second-guessing? _____

_____

_____

_____

_____

3) Were there any gifts/callings that you are now second-guessing? _____Yes _____ No

If so, what are they and why are you second-guessing? _____

_____

_____

_____

_____

4) Were there any gifts/callings that you are now second-guessing? _____Yes _____ No

If so, what are they and why are you second-guessing? _____

_____

_____

_____

CHAPTER 8
HOMEWORK

1. Do you have any gifts that was not mentioned? _____ Yes _____ No _____ Unsure

What are those gifts? _____

_____

_____

_____

_____

2. How do you know you have those gifts? _____

_____

_____

_____

_____

CHAPTER 9

Your Ministry Bio

It is time to tell the world who you are. Your ministry bio states your qualifications, your education, your experience, your purpose, and your vision. It is a spiritual autobiography that reflects your spiritual journey. It reflects your individual beliefs, experiences, education, and your life achievements.

You should share 4 main elements in your ministry biography. They are as follows:

1) What you do

2) Why you do what you do

3) What makes you qualified to do what you do

4) Personal details about yourself

To be more precise your ministry biography should include the following:

1) A personal summary of who you are

2) All of the volunteer work you have done in the church

3) Any missionary trips you have been on

4) List your education

5) List your ministry experience

6) Express a personal statement of salvation

7) Make mention of your family life if you want to share

Your ministry biography shares with the world who you are before they even meet you.

HOMEWORK

1) Search the internet for your ministry biography samples.

2) Share a pastor's ministry biography.

3) Work on completing your ministry biography.

4) Your final ministry biography should be typed and include a picture of you.

CHAPTER 10

Final Self-Evaluation

Now that you have completed the course and searched the scripture, it's time to do one final evaluation. Please answer the following questions:

1) What steps will you take to abide by God's word in your calling? _____

_____

_____

_____

_____

_____

_____

_____

_____

2) What further training will you seek? _____

_____

_____

_____

_____

_____

_____

_____

_____

_____

_____

3) What ministry do you feel will make the greatest impact in your world? _____

_____

_____

_____

_____

_____

_____

_____

_____

_____

4) Now that you've completed the course, what additional thoughts do you have? _____

_____

_____

_____

_____

_____

_____

_____

_____

_____

_____

_____

5) Who is the mentor that you can talk to and get further spiritual leadership? _____

_____

_____

_____

_____

_____

_____

_____

_____

_____

_____

6) What insights have you gained from this course? _____

_____

_____

_____

_____

_____

_____

_____

7) What questions do you have? _____

_____

_____

_____

_____

_____

_____

_____

8) What has changed for you since taking this course? _____

_____

_____

_____

_____

_____

VOCABULARY WORDS

Accept   Consent to receive something offered. *Psalm 119:108*

Anointing   The supernatural power of God. *Isaiah 10:27*

Call   A summons from God to operate spiritually with the leading of the Holy Spirit. With that call is the empowerment and effectiveness of gifts that were already placed in the believer to participate in God's redemptive work in the work. *Acts 9:3-9*

Calling   A strong urge toward a particular way of life. *Judges 6:8-23*

Heard   To be told or informed of. *Romans 10:17*

Humility   A modest or low view of one's importance: Not proud and one who does not believe they are better than other people. *Colossians 3:12-13*

Niche   A comfortable or suitable position in life. *Acts 1:8*

Purpose   It declares why you exist. Your purpose defines your life – not in terms of what you think but what God knows. It anchors your life in the character and calling of God. *Psalm 57:2*

Supernatural   Attributed to a force beyond human capability and scientific understanding. It goes against the laws of nature. *Ephesians 3:20*

Vocation   A divine call to God's service or to the life of identifying as a Christian. A function or station in life to which one is called by God. *Ephesians 4:1*

JOURNALING

Date: _____

_____

_____

_____

_____

_____

_____

Date: _____

_____

_____

_____

_____

Date: _____

Date: _____

Date: _____

Date: _____

Date: _____

Date: _____

Date: _____

_____

_____

_____

_____

_____

Date: _____

_____

_____

_____

_____

Date: _____

_____

REFERENCES

King James Bible Dictionary (2024). Bible Verses. Retrieved from https://biblegen.com

Ligonier Ministries (2005). Make your election sure. Retrieved from https://www.ligonier.org

Wagner, P. (2016). Finding your spiritual gifts the easy-to-use self-guided questionnaire. Chosen Baker Publishing Group.